THE SOUTH HAMS

A shortish gu

Amanda Richar

GW00503962

Bossiney Books · Launceston

First published 2009 by Bossiney Books Ltd
Langore, Launceston, Cornwall PL15 8LD
www.bossineybooks.com
ISBN 978-1-906474-15-7
Acknowledgements
The maps are by Graham Hallowell
The cover is based on a design by Heards Design Partnership
All photographs are from the publishers' own collection
Printed in Great Britain by R Booth Ltd, Penryn, Cornwall

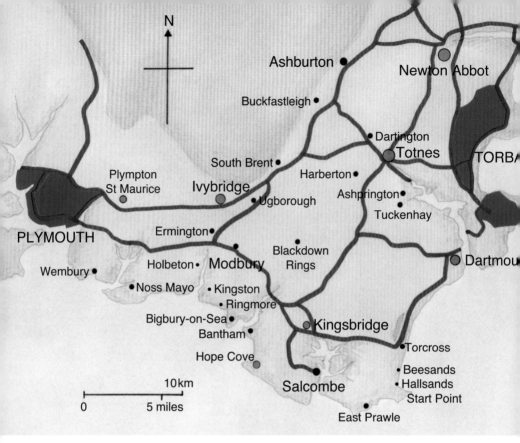

Contents

Introduction

The area of Devon covered in this guide lies south of the A38 and between the rivers Plym and Dart. It is popularly known as 'the South Hams', a very ancient name, though historically its limits were never precisely defined and its parishes extended to the borders of Dartmoor. (The South Hams District Council has slightly different borders, for reasons both of history and of administrative convenience when it was founded in 1974.) There probably never was a 'North Hams'.

The historic towns of the South Hams are the river ports of Totnes and Kingsbridge, the seaport of Dartmouth, and the smaller town of Modbury. We have also included a description of the medieval castle town of Plympton St Maurice. Salcombe, now a small town, developed from a village only after 1800, as did the mill town of Ivybridge, which lies just outside our area.

The majority of the 80,000 population still live in villages or even smaller settlements. The landscape is characterised by rounded hills, red soils and narrow lanes with high hedges. It is an area with a rich agricultural, industrial and military heritage. There are time-worn drovers' paths, archaic field systems, quarries, limestone kilns and old mills of all kinds dotted around – though unfortunately not many are working now.

What brings many visitors to the area is the stunning coastline, 100km of it, of which around 26km are beaches. There are dramatic seascapes and fabulous coastal walks. Landing stages and quays, once suited to an international maritime trade, are located along the five river estuaries of the Yealm, Avon, Erme, Kingsbridge-Salcombe and the Dart. Defensive fortifications are sited throughout the district, spanning all ages from pre-history to WW2. Along the coast, there are fishing villages, smugglers' haunts and myriad tales of wrecking, piracy and raids by Barbary slave traders.

This short guide can only highlight a few of the places of interest in the South Hams. There are many more special places to seek out and explore. Enjoy your journey!

Opening times

Please note that opening dates and times vary from year to year. 'Seasonal opening' usually means from Good Friday or 1 April, whichever is earlier, to end October – best check before visiting.

Totnes

Totnes nestles in the rounded hills of South Devon, by the uppermost navigable reaches of the River Dart. Idiosyncratic in nature and with a reputation for a relaxed bohemian culture, there really is no other town in Devon like it – steeped in history yet cosmopolitan and forward-looking.

The main thoroughfare of Fore Street leading up to High Street gives Totnes much of its obvious character and charm. There are intriguing passageways from which you get tantalising glimpses of hidden courtyards and houses beyond. Many of the buildings on this thoroughfare are mediaeval, some with later false frontages, but the prevailing feeling is of times gone by. Despite 20th century traffic, it is not hard to imagine Elizabethan men and women going about their business. The iconic East Gate Arch is Totnes' best known landmark. It burned down in a fire in 1990. Now lovingly replaced, it still spans the main street and divides Fore Street from High Street.

Top right: Totnes is well known for its excellent markets. These are held in the Civic Square and Civic Hall on Fridays and Saturdays. People also come to see the small Elizabethan Charity and Craft Market on Tuesday mornings in the summer months, when stall-holders dress in Tudor costume

Middle: Tucked behind the impressive 14th century red sandstone parish church of St Mary, on the ancient Ramparts Walk, lies the Totnes Guildhall, often missed by visitors. Currently housing the Town Council and its offices, the Guildhall has been significant to the town for nearly a thousand years. It has had a variety of incarnations, ranging from a priory to a magistrates court, and its fascinating history is displayed all around you in a disarmingly casual way when you visit the building. Seasonal opening

Bottom: The Norman motte-and-bailey castle

A view over the ancient centre of Totnes

Totnes Museum is based in a Tudor merchant's house, dating from around 1575. As well as locally significant exhibits, the Museum celebrates Charles Babbage, inventor of the first computer, and William Wills, the Australian explorer – both with strong connections with the town. Seasonal opening.

Further up the main street, in part of the colonnaded Butterwalk, Bogan House hosts the Devonshire Collection of Period Costume. This building also has a fine decorative plaster ceiling.

At the highest point in the town Totnes Castle is a Norman motte-and-bailey (English Heritage, seasonal opening). There are panoramic vistas of Totnes and the River Dart from the ramparts.

Although most of the museums are seasonal, one of the delights of the town at any time of year is wandering up the main street, visiting the many small independent shops, and people-watching from one of the cafés. Totnes has long been known for its 'alternative culture' and boasts several centres for complementary medicine and health food shops which are a magnet for visitors.

'The Narrows' at the top of the town, which was once closely confined by its wall. The original circuit of the wall is easy to see on a map, and to explore on foot

The Leechwells, near the medieval Kingsbridge Inn, are reputed to have medicinal properties. The three springs are called the Snake, the Toad, and the Long Crippler – but no one can say authoritatively which is which!

More recently, Totnes has become one of the founder 'Transition Towns' – a movement which aims to secure a future after oil begins to run out. It has also achieved, partly through Radio 4's *The Archers*, national publicity for its own currency – the Totnes Pound. The Pound was launched in 2007 and it is possible to buy and spend them in a number of businesses in the town. Many people simply save one as a souvenir.

Totnes has a thriving nightlife for a town of its size. There are a number of historic public houses, and the hotel and several other bars offer music. One or two also offer a resident ghost.

The River Dart remains the focus of many activities in Totnes. Near the river, at the bottom of Fore Street, is the restored Town Mill. The Mill is the current home of the Information Centre and of the Totnes Image Bank, which catalogues thousands of images from Totnes, Dartington and the wider surrounding area.

The tidal waterwheel at the Mill is operational, thanks to the historic leat which runs from Totnes weir on the River Dart. Sadly, the Mill no longer grinds corn and the waterwheel cannot at the moment provide power for the occupants. Moves are afoot to consider how the water power could be harnessed and, on a larger scale, whether the weir could be used to generate power for Totnes.

Kingswear Station, looking towards Dartmouth. Steam trains connect Kingswear with Paignton, as part of the 'Round Robin' trip

The Dart is a beautiful river with an incredible history and complex ecology, as the 1 1/4 hour trip along its lower reaches to the sea reveals. There are seasonal ferries between Totnes and Dartmouth, at the mouth of the Dart, which usually run between April and October. As the river is tidal, timings change on a daily basis. In season, it is also possible to do a circular trip by boat, steam train and bus. Known as 'the Round Robin', this connects Totnes with Dartmouth and Paignton. It can be a spectacular way to spend a day and provides an excellent overview of the history of the area. Totnes is also one end of the South Devon Steam Railway (see page 27).

Short walks from Totnes

The level walk to Dartington Cider Press Centre (2.8km or 1 3/4 miles each way from Totnes bridge) can be extended across the Dartington Estate to take in Dartington Hall and its stunning grounds (for this route, see *Really short walks – South Devon*).

Another level walk on the opposite side of the river leads past Steamer Quay beyond the Rowing Club and onto Longmarsh – the old Rifle Range, now a conservation area. Though a bit prone to flooding at the highest tides, and consequently suffering some damage, the path is accessible to wheelchairs and buggies.

The walk from Totnes to Ashprington, about 4km each way, can be turned into a 'circular' route by utilising the footpath in one direction and the purpose-built cycleway in the other.

Dartmouth's Embankment, a perfect place to stroll or to sit and watch the activity on the river

The 'Boat Float' with the Royal Castle Hotel ahead, and Royal Avenue Gardens to the right

Dartmouth

Passengers disembarking from visiting cruise ships have compared Dartmouth to the glamorous Italian haunt of the stars, Portofino. The scramble of multi-coloured buildings that compose Dartmouth and its opposite settlement of Kingswear seem to cling to either side of the hilly, densely wooded estuary.

Because a companion book in this series, *Dartmouth – a Shortish Guide*, is devoted to the town, Dartmouth will receive less space in this book than it otherwise would. It is essentially a 12th century port town with narrow medieval streets and many ancient buildings – not a few occupied by art galleries – and there is much to explore.

9

There are several ways to reach Dartmouth – from Paignton by steam train and ferry, from Totnes by river, or by road. Parking can be a problem and a visit by car in summer will almost inevitably mean using the park-and-ride, on the upper edge of town beside the A3122 near Sainsburys. The park-and-ride bus, though, will deliver you right to the centre of Dartmouth. As you step off onto The Embankment, pause to look across the small square boat marina (known locally as 'the Boat Float') to the Butterwalk – the timber-frame building jettied out on stone columns – and the historic Royal Castle Hotel.

The Embankment, approximately 800 m (1/2 mile) long, provides a level, fascinating walk next to the river. At the seaward end, a little beyond the Lower Ferry, is Bayards Cove (photograph below) with its Tudor fort. Look out to the mouth of the Dart, towards Dartmouth Castle.

From the South Embankment, in the season, it is possible to take a ferry to the steps below the Castle, which was built around 1490 to defend the town and harbour. A chain could be strung across the harbour entrance, and the Castle (now English Heritage, fee) was designed to mount artillery. There are walks around the Castle area and out along the South West Coast Path to Little Dartmouth and beyond. The coastal route is strenuous in parts but beautiful. From the Castle you can either walk back to the town centre (about 1.6 km, 1 mile, fairly easy walking) or return on the ferry.

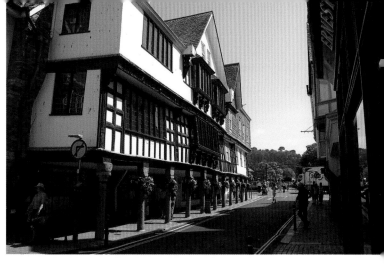

The Butterwalk, four timber-frame houses built around 1640. The Dartmouth Heritage Museum occupies the house nearest the river

As you walk along the South Embankment, past cafés and restaurants, note a restaurant positioned right on the Embankment opposite the 'Boat Float'. This is the old Dartmouth railway station, thought to be unique in that it has never welcomed a train. The broad gauge Dartmouth & Torbay Railway was meant to terminate at Dartmouth but this never happened. Instead, the line ended at Kingswear and passengers then took the ferry to Dartmouth, as they still do.

Across the road are the Royal Avenue Gardens. The success of tender plants in the Gardens, such as olive trees in the Mediterranean section and New Zealand tree ferns, is evidence of Dartmouth's sheltered climate. Near the Gardens and just inside the car park is Dartmouth Tourist Information Centre and the Thomas Newcomen Engine. Newcomen, the inventor of the steam engine, was born in Dartmouth in 1663 and plied his original trade as an ironmonger here. The particular beam engine on display was built around the end of the 18th century and was used by the Coventry Canal Company. It still works and can be viewed for free.

From the Embankment you are bound to notice the amount of activity on the river. Ferries, ocean-going yachts and small boats will be coming and going. Cruise ships, military vessels, tall ships – Dartmouth sees them all. There will be children crabbing and fishing from the Embankment in the summer. Occasionally the river may seem to 'boil' as fish are chased in a circle by visiting seals.

As you reach Coronation Park, look up to see Britannia Royal Naval College peering imperiously over the trees. Until it opened in 1905, officers of the Royal Navy lived and trained in cramped conditions in two wooden ships moored in the river.

Salcombe

On a summer's day you could easily spend hours just watching the activity in the estuary from one of Salcombe's many handy harbour-side benches – boats, tenders and ferries buzz about. It is another South Devon hot-spot for crabbing. Families cluster round crab lines on the embankment, just round the corner from the Salcombe Lifeboat Station and Museum in Union Street. This is an RNLI 'Explore Station' and is normally open to visitors 10-4.30 daily.

The narrow main street through Salcombe, though small, has a variety of up-market clothing and gift shops and a range of eateries. Salcombe also produces its own delicious ice cream, a 'must-seek-out' pleasure on any visit.

While the town hums in summer it is much more sedate in the winter months. Weather-wise, Salcombe doesn't have a winter season. As a consequence, the whole area is a gardener's delight with many examples of unusual sub-tropical and tender plants to be found.

Salcombe Maritime Museum (open daily April – October) occupies two rooms beneath the Information Centre in the former Council Offices. It has a small but diverting collection of local historic items, including over thirty ship portraits from the 19th century, and salvage from the many wrecks that have happened along the coast. From Salcombe or the small settlement of East Portlemouth opposite (reached by ferry) walkers can join the South West Coast Path to explore both sides of the Estuary and beyond.

Overbeck's Museum and Garden (National Trust)

Situated near the coastal path in a cliff-top setting just outside Salcombe, Overbeck's is an Edwardian house with wonderful views of the estuary and the coastline. Until 1937 it was owned by scientist, inventor and collector Otto Overbeck. His idiosyncratic collections of natural history, nautical artefacts and curios are on display in the house, alongside the intriguing yet somewhat disturbing electrical apparatus he invented to promote youth: 'The Rejuvenator'.

The sheltered climatic conditions that prevail at Salcombe have produced a lush garden at Overbeck's now managed on organic principles. The garden is open throughout the year but closed on certain days of the week, according to the season.

Top: Salcombe is blessed with an idyllic setting on the Kingsbridge Estuary. It has a mild climate and its golden beaches are within easy reach of the town centre

Below: Kingsbridge harbour at high tide

Kingsbridge

Kingsbridge is a bustling market town with a strong trading and maritime tradition, located at the head of the flooded ria valley which is called the Kingsbridge Estuary. In the summer months, depending on the tide, there are daily ferries between Kingsbridge and Salcombe.

Like many towns in South Devon, Kingsbridge is built on a hill. The main thoroughfare, Fore Street, whilst requiring some stamina to walk up, holds plenty of interest with a variety of independent shops and businesses. Also located on this street is the Cookworthy Museum of Rural Life, named after William Cookworthy, an apothecary from Kingsbridge, hailed as the father of the English porcelain industry. Open March to September, the nine galleries and collections in the museum focus on the social history of Kingsbridge and its environs.

Modbury

Modbury is positioned on the A379 – at the junction of the old roads from Dartmouth and from Kingsbridge to Plymouth. It is a small town with a population of about 1500 and has a quiet, rather genteel feel. It was mentioned in *Domesday Book* and is believed to date back further as a Saxon meeting place – 'Moot-burgh'.

In 2007 it achieved national fame as the first town to have become entirely plastic-bag free. It has an interesting main street with small independent shops and businesses.

Modbury Heritage Project has located a number of notable historic sites in the town, which are identified by mounted brass plaques. The oldest surviving inn in Modbury is the Exeter Inn, parts of which date from the 14th century. The streets most worth exploring are Church Street, leading from the Exeter Inn up the hill towards Plymouth, and Brownston Street, the old Dartmouth road, which has a number of interesting old houses, notably 'Traine' at the top of the hill, built in 1780 so rather modern by Modbury standards.

The town was the scene of a battle in the Civil Wars: in 1642 2000 Royalists dug in and tried to prevent 8000 Parliamentarians from advancing on Plymouth. They held out for nine hours, before making a well-organised retreat along the old road to Plymouth, now rather unfairly known as Runaway Lane. If you want to see what medieval Devon roads were like, this is a good example. Wellies recommended!

Plympton St Maurice

This little medieval castle town lies north of the A38, just outside the area covered, but such an unknown gem that we decided to include it.

Approaching from the east on the A38, take the PLYMPTON exit and turn right towards Plympton. At a roundabout, turn left. Shortly before another roundabout, turn left, New Park Road. Continue ahead along Long Cause. Approaching the church, find on-street parking.

Now walk ahead into Barbican Road. Bear left at the war memorial into the castle grounds (free). After exploring the castle remains, continue through the grounds and out to Fore Street. It is worth turning right and walking a little way along, before retracing your steps along Fore Street. Take the second left, which passes the impressive seventeenth century former Grammar School. The artist Sir Joshua Reynolds was born in a house on this site.

Plympton Castle is a Norman motte-and-bailey built in the 12th century by the Earls of Devon to protect their manor of Plympton. The shell keep, now largely ruined, was the only keep in Devon where timbers were used to re-inforce the wall, and evidence of this still remains. The castle fell into disrepair in the 15th century. By the 19th century, the bailey was being used for village events such as fairs, circuses and maypole dancing.

Some South Hams villages

For many visitors, part of the pleasure of south Devon consists of not doing very much! Here is a selection of villages worthy of a quiet stroll, and where (at the time of writing) you will find a pub or two.

Ugborough (top left)

Ugborough has a village square with plenty of parking and a restored Victorian conduit which until 1942 served as the first piped water supply to the village. The church of St Peter dominates the Square. The north aisle has some curious roof bosses, including a Green Man.

Ermington (middle left)

Ermington has an ancient holy well, a church with a crooked spire (rebuilt in stone in the 19th century to preserve its crookedness) and a pub called, strangely enough, 'The Crooked Spire'.

Kingston (bottom left)

The 16th century Dolphin Inn at Kingston has a unique sign 'please drive slowly through the pub'.

Ringmore (top right)

Ringmore is lovely village where thatched cottages abound. From the 'Ayrmer Cove' car park there is a level walk out to the cliffs, with wonderful views over Ayrmer Cove and towards Burgh Island (see lower photo on page 18) in the opposite direction. There are a number of other good walks – see *Really short walks South Devon*.

Ashprington
A picturesque village on the Dart Valley Trail, just south of Totnes.

Tuckenhay
Sedate Tuckenhay, on Bow Creek, was once very different – a thriving industrial centre. Its paper mill, famed for producing quality paper suitable for banknotes, is now a complex of self-catering holiday cottages. There are walks along the Creek but parking is tricky in the village itself.

Harberton (middle right)
The houses and cottages in Harberton cluster around narrow jumbled streets in a lush, hilly setting. The medieval Church House Inn and its neighbour St Andrew's Church provide a focus. Church houses originated as a type of community building in the Middle Ages. In Devon many examples remain and some are public houses, hence the popularity of the name '(Old) Church House Inn' in the county.

East Prawle
East Prawle is Devon's most southerly village, full of character. The Pig's Nose, the village pub, is a well known focal point, and the Prawle Point lookout station a popular destination for a stroll.

Holbeton
A traditional yet lively picture-postcard village with two pubs.

Starting from East Prawle, there are wonderful coastal walks – for example to Elender Bay

Burgh Island from Bigbury-on-Sea, with the sea tractor in operation

Burgh Island from near Ringmore, where a level footpath leads from the Ayrmer Cove car park, giving wonderful views in both directions (see page 16)

Bigbury-on-Sea and Burgh Island

Bigbury-on-Sea has a popular family beach, with lifeguards during the summer, a café and a shop. The sandy beach can get very crowded at peak times and at high tide the usable area can diminish to a small triangle. There are a couple of car parks nearby.

A visit to Bigbury-on-Sea is not really complete without a short trip over to the memorable Burgh Island, across the sandy tidal causeway. Time your arrival with high tide and use the unique sea tractor for a small charge or walk across the causeway when low tide allows.

Once on the island, there is a short walk on the public footpath past the Pilchard Inn across to Herring Cove, a tiny rocky inlet. The visible ruin at the summit of the island is believed to be a huer's hut. A huer was a lookout who signalled the approach of shoals of pilchards to waiting fishermen, then directed the boats as they encircled the fish.

The Pilchard Inn is the historic island pub, established in 1336 and patronised over the centuries by fishermen, smugglers and latterly visitors. Now owned by the hotel, only one bar is open to the general public.

Hope Cove

Protected by the promontory of Bolt Tail, Hope Cove consists of two settlements: Inner and Outer Hope. Like many coastal villages in the area, Hope Cove was once famous for fishing, especially for pilchards at Quay Cove, and has a dark smuggling past.

In modern times it is better known as a family holiday destination and for its sheltered beaches. A visit to the village in summer reveals a plethora of small boats hauled up in the cove or bobbing around on the sea, and families enjoying beach games. There is good and easy access to facilities such as pubs and restaurants.

There are interesting coastal walks to be done from here. To the south is Bolt Tail, with its iron age hillfort and magnificent views. To the north are less arduous walks to Thurlestone Sands and freshwater South Milton Ley. The whole area is excellent for birdwatching.

From this part of the coast on a clear day, there are views of the famous Eddystone Lighthouse, lying 13 miles south west of Plymouth, with the stump of the earlier Smeaton's Tower next to it. The upper section of Smeaton's Tower has been re-erected on Plymouth Hoe.

Wembury Bay and Marine Centre

Wembury beach is in a Marine Conservation Area and is a must for those interested in marine life of the south Devon coast. The Marine Centre is located on the edge of Wembury National Trust car park and entry is free. Seasonal opening, variable hours: tel 01752 862538. The Centre organises a variety of events, including rock pool rambles. There is an accessible exhibition of 'life on the seashore' in the Centre and an educational film of the wildlife that inhabits the waters which includes dolphins, porpoises, octopus and basking sharks. There are also two small marine tanks in the Centre.

Wembury Bay supports a range of bird life. Peregrine falcons and oystercatchers frequent the beaches and stonechats, Dartford warblers and cirl bunting are found in the scrubland along the cliffs. The Great Mew Stone, clearly visible off Wembury, hosts the most important cormorant and shag colony in south-west England.

Wembury beach, though small and rocky, is scenic and popular with experienced surfers.

The National Trust own the Old Mill which buttresses the beach, historically a water mill used to grind grain, now a café. There is also a shop, selling beach gear. St Werburgh's Church, with its 14th century tower, is a dominant feature above the beach. There are stunning walks along the coastal path in both directions.

Noss Mayo

This picturesque village of narrow cottage-lined streets lies to the south of the tidal Newton Creek, opposite the larger settlement of Newton Ferrers and close to the mouth of the River Yealm. Residents traditionally made their living by farming and fishing; now it is a haven for leisure yachts.

There is practically no on-street parking in Noss. Instead, park for free at the car park on the edge of Brooking's Down Wood. (Bear right at the church, down Revelstoke Road, and continue ahead at the junction.) There are circular walks around these woods and an array of wildlife to be spotted: you will find a good information board on the edge of the car park. There are two inns: the Ship and the Swan. Both overlook the creek and have outdoor seating areas.

From Slapton Ley to Start Point

The 'Lower Ley' at Slapton (photograph below) is the largest natural lake in south-west England, thought to be more than 3000 years old and created by the natural damning of an estuary.

The 3km shingle ridge dividing the lagoon from the sea has been pushed up by rising sea levels in the 10,000 years since the most recent ice age. It is a nationally important example of a 'bay bar'.

The marshes, reed beds and woodland that surround the Ley all contribute to a habitat which has extraordinary flora and fauna. It is particularly important for passage and wintering birds. Although it is a Site of Special Scientific Interest, much of the area is accessible to the public. There is a lot to see in every season. Footpaths around the site are shown on information boards at several access points

Slapton Ley Field Centre is open all year round. It offers a range of courses and a programme of more informal guided walks through the seasons, led either by staff or volunteers. There is usually a charge made and booking is essential.

Torcross

Torcross, at the southern end of the lake, has several shops and places to eat, including the Start Bay Inn, a family-run pub well known for its fish and chips and its seafood menu. There is limited on-street parking, as well as at Torcross Lay-by and further along the A379 at

Looking south over Widdicombe Ley to Beesands, and Start Point beyond

the Sherman Tank. This American tank took part in the ill-fated D-day Exercise Tiger practice landings at Slapton Beach in 1944, where hundreds of American service men lost their lives, and was lost at sea until its recovery in 1984. It commemorates the men who participated in these exercises. Another memorial further north along the beach is dedicated to the local people who were obliged to move from their homes and farms.

Beesands

Beesands is a small linear village behind a lengthy shingle beach – a fishing community dating back at least to the early nineteenth century. Single-man fishing boats are hauled up on the beach and a row of fishermen's cottages lines the road. Protected from the worst ravages of the sea by a robust sea wall and recently re-fortified defences, it is still well known for fishing. Start Bay crabs and other locally landed fish can be bought from an outlet on the spot. The beach is a choice haunt for amateur anglers too. Car parking is free.

Tourism is the main income generator now but even at the height of summer the village maintains a tranquil, away-from-it-all air. There is a small but lively pub and a warm and welcoming chapel, St Andrew's Church, which is one of very few churches still remaining in regular use so close to the sea. The freshwater Widdicombe Ley, an important wildlife site, lies to the north of the village.

Hallsands seen from Start Point

Hallsands

The walk from Beesands to Hallsands along the cliff path is just 2 km. Hallsands is the notorious ruined village between Beesands and Start Point. On 26 January 1917 the deadly combination of a severe storm from the east, pounding waves and high tides led to the destruction and desertion of the village. Only two houses now remain intact.

There is no access to the old village but there is a viewing platform above it, with information boards which explain the history and reasons for the village's demise. The whole area is deeply atmospheric, especially when the sea mist rolls in and the fog horn at Start Point blows. There is no public parking at South Hallsands.

Start Point

Single track roads lead slowly to the dramatic and rocky Start Point, described as being one of the most exposed peninsulas in England. There is a private car park where a charge is payable – this car park also gives access to Great Mattiscombe Sand (see page 31). It is a short walk to Start Point Lighthouse, located right on the promontory. Operated by Trinity House, the lighthouse is open for guided tours at certain times of the year, weather permitting, and for a small charge.

It is also straightforward to reach Start Point by walking along the coast path from the north. On a good day, there are beautiful views of Start Bay from this section of the coast path.

Dartington

The Dartington Hall Estate, managed by the Dartington Hall Trust, lies just over 3km north of Totnes. It has a thousand year history but in its present form it was the project of Dorothy and Leonard Elmhirst, who bought the ruined estate in 1925. Together they created a progressive model for educational, social and rural experimentation, which in turn over the years attracted many creative and well known artists and musicians. The Estate is home to places of learning and to international literary and music events throughout the year.

The Great Hall and Courtyard

The original manor house at Dartington was built in 1388 by the half brother of Richard II, John Holland, Earl of Huntingdon and Duke of Exeter. The Great Hall and Courtyard formed part of this house. Today, the Great Hall and Courtyard complex is used year round as a hotel, as a wedding venue, for conferences and for arts performances. It is possible to wander for free around the Courtyard and look into the Great Hall itself, provided it is not in use.

The White Hart Bar and Dining Room is situated next to the Great Hall and is a good place to stop for a light bite and coffee or a more substantial meal. There is also a small coffee bar next to the Barn, a performance space and independent cinema near the Courtyard.

High Cross House

Described as a modernist architectural gem, High Cross House was designed by the famous Swiss-American architect Willem Lecaze. High Cross House is open to the general public May to October on a restricted basis: there is a small charge for entry.

The gardens and grounds

The gardens are a delightful, peaceful space and a perfect antidote to the busy wider world. They are open dawn to dusk, all year round. A donation is encouraged at the entrance to the estate to help maintain the gardens.

Call at reception when you arrive and you can collect a map of the gardens and a brief guide to the history and architecture of the estate. Limited sections of the gardens are accessible to those with mobility problems and again a map showing routes can be collected at reception. No dogs are allowed in the Courtyard and gardens, except guide dogs. Guided tours are available by arrangement for a fee.

In early spring, Dartington is well known locally for the profusion of crocuses which bravely poke their heads up under tree canopies in the garden. Several fine and intriguing sculptures are scattered around the grounds, including one by Henry Moore.

Rambling around other parts of the Dartington Estate is possible. There are a few waymarked public footpaths through the grounds, mainly woodland paths. Other paths also exist. These are permissive and there is no absolute legal right of way. They may close at short notice.

Other interesting local gardens

Hamblyn's Coombe near Dittisham is a 3 hectare garden belonging to sculptor Bridget McCrum. Sited on the River Dart opposite the Greenway estate, the garden has glorious views and magnificent colours in autumn. It is open for a small fee as part of the National Garden Scheme. Lovely sculptures, bronzes and stone carvings intermingle easily with interesting garden design features. Visitors are welcome all year by appointment, except in July and August. Tel: 01803 722228.

Blackpool Gardens is a relatively recently restored 19th century subtropical garden, near Blackpool Sands, with wonderful views of Start Bay. Open May to October. Adults pay a small charge but children go in free. Park in the car park at Blackpool Sands.

The South Devon Railway

The South Devon Railway branch line, opened in May 1872, originally ran between Ashburton and Totnes. Following a period of steady commercial decline, the line eventually closed in 1962. Re-opened several years later, it is now a successful preserved steam line and in season runs from Totnes Littlehempston Station (about 500 m from Totnes mainline station across the River Dart), to Buckfastleigh.

From central Totnes, roughly two hours either side of high tide, it may be possible to catch the small passenger ferry, *The River Rat*, to take you up-river to the steam railway. Departing from Vire Island or the Steam Packet Inn, this enjoyable short trip is an alternative to the twenty minute wooded riverside walk from Totnes Bridge.

On the opposite side of the line to Littlehempston Station is another of Totnes's newer attractions, the Totnes Rare Breeds Farm, which hosts a delightful selection of animals you can feed including goats, pigs and rare sheep. For many, their most interesting guests are the owls, ranging from Little Owls to Eagle Owls, and they are fortunate to have several impressive species you can handle – under close supervision, of course. Seasonal opening.

At the Buckfastleigh end of the line, there are several attractions, all seasonal. On the same site as the station is Buckfast Butterflies and Otter Sanctuary. There is also a vintage bus ride into Buckfastleigh (to visit the Valiant Soldier) and Buckfast Abbey.

Dittisham

A very desirable place to live or to have a second home, with property prices to match, this exquisite Devon village is located in a stunning setting on the River Dart, about 5 km from Dartmouth. The Ham is the easiest and most atmospheric place to park – follow the signs once you enter the village. From The Ham, take a moment to gaze out at the widest part of the River Dart, known locally as Broad Reach or Dittisham Lake. The open water stretches over 1.5 km at high tide.

If the tide permits, take the short walk from The Ham along the foreshore to the Quay and the Ferry Boat Inn. Watch out for herons, little egrets, cormorants, kingfishers and oystercatchers. At high tide, use the footpath at the far back boundary of The Ham. This is a 5-10 minute walk, uphill for the most part but downhill sharply at the end. Follow the signs for the Quay, and the Ferry Boat Inn will be on your left.

There has been a ferry at this point of the river for more than a thousand years. The Dittisham-Greenway Ferry operates year round, weather permitting, and can still be summoned by ringing the bell on either side of the river. For bookings and enquiries tel: 01803 844010.

Greenway, now owned by the National Trust, was Agatha Christie's summer home. It is a short but steep walk from Greenway Quay to the property. The garden is open from March to October but is at its most stunning on a lovely late spring day. By 2009, Agatha Christie's house should also be open to the public.

The Blackdown Rings and Andrew's Wood

The Blackdown Rings (grid reference SX 719521) are an impressive Iron Age hillfort more than 2000 years old, with the remains of a much later Norman motte-and-bailey castle in the north-west corner of the old earthworks. The 5 hectare site is owned by the Arundell Charity, who restored it and now allow free public access.

Located off the B3196, between California Cross and the village of Loddiswell, the site is a bit tricky to find but well worth the effort. Driving south, turn left at Blackdown Cross. Drive up this lane and after 500 m (¹/₃ mile) there is a small car park on the right, signed with an ancient monument symbol.

Andrew's Wood, managed by Devon Wildlife Trust, is within striking distance of the Blackdown Rings, either by walking along lanes and a footpath or by driving to the small car park on site. The woodland is mainly birch and is less than 60 years old but provides a lovely setting for an afternoon ramble.

There is an information board near the car park (grid reference SX 713520) and the trails are waymarked. Andrew's Wood is one of only three sites in Britain where you can see the rare Heath Lobelia and it is also well known for orchids. It would not be unusual to see nuthatches, greater spotted woodpeckers, long tailed tits, buzzards and silver-washed fritillary butterflies. However, keep to the trails as the site has deep ditches, marshy areas and fallen trees.

Bantham has a reputation as one of the best surfing beaches in South Devon, so can be busy. There is plentiful parking, for which there is a charge. Lifeguards monitor the beach in summer. Other facilities are very limited

A small selection of beaches

The Erme Estuary – Mothecombe and Wonwell

Mothecombe is a fine private beach owned by the Flete Estate, open to visitors on Wednesdays, Saturdays and Sundays. The car park is open all year and it is also a good starting point for coast path walking. The walk from the car park to Meadowsfoot beach is about 400m, along an access path, and it offers lovely sand and rockpools. The estuary beach at the end of Mothecombe Slipway, near the Old Coastguard Cottages, is a little nearer, at the end of a tarmac lane.

There are no beach facilities but there is a tea shop in the car park, open Easter to mid September. Toilets are located here too.

The River Erme can be forded on foot an hour either side of low tide from the beach below the Old Coastguard cottages, as part of the South West Coast Path, to reach Wonwell Beach. Otherwise, road access to Wonwell is extremely limited.

Bantham

Bantham is a beautiful, rural, sandy beach at the mouth of the River Avon, overlooking Burgh Island and backed by dunes.

Thurlestone

Thurlestone Sand and its near neighbour Leas Foot Sand are large enough to support a variety of activities, such as windsurfing, kayaking, kite flying and swimming, even at the height of the season. Lifeguards monitor Thurlestone between July and September. Thurlestone Rock, a stranded arch composed of new red sandstone, provides visual and geological interest. At low tide there is potential for rockpooling.

Great Mattiscombe is inaccessible by car, so is often much quieter than its beauty should really allow. It involves a short but steep walk on a public footpath across fields from Start Point car park, or a scramble along the coastal path

Blackpool Sands is a privately managed family beach, just over 1 km long, with a lush woodland backdrop (see also page 26)

South Milton Sands National Trust car park is located right behind Thurlestone beach, but some access routes to the sand are steep. There is another privately run car park to the north. Dogs are allowed.

Lannacombe beach
A lovely rural beach. Unlike its neighbour, Great Mattiscombe, it can be reached by car and consequently is popular with locals. However, access is by a narrow lane and parking is very limited.

Great Mattiscombe Sand
An unspoilt beach along the coast from Start Point – see photo above.

Blackpool Sands
Blackpool Sands has good facilities which include toilets, a café, lifeguards in summer, opportunities for watersports and plentiful parking (for which there is a charge). The beach is coarse sand with some fine shingle, cleaned on a daily basis in the summer. No dogs allowed on the beach or in the car park.

South Sands beach at Salcombe, where there is a car park and other facilities. It can be reached by ferry from Salcombe, or by walking, but the road is narrow so you would need to take care. North Sands beach is easier to access.

Useful Information

Dartmouth Tourist Information Centre   01803 834224
Kingsbridge Information Centre   01548 853195
Modbury Tourist Information Centre   01548 830159
Salcombe Tourist Information Centre   01548 843927
Totnes Tourist Information Centre   01803 863168

The area is covered by Ordnance Survey Explorer map OL20 which is two sided, so excellent value.

Walking in South Devon

South Devon is a great place for walking and Bossiney Books is a specialist walks book publisher. May we recommend

Really short walks – South Devon (3-5km walks)
Shortish walks – the south Devon Coast (5-8km walks)
Shortish walks – Torbay and Dartmouth (5-8km walks)
Really short walks – South Dartmoor (3-5km walks)
